GIFT
GOD RUNS THROUGH ALL THESE ROOMS

Duane Vorhees

```
Hog Press
918 5TH ST
Ames, IA 50010
USA
hogpress.com
editor@hogpress.com
+1 (352) 388-3848
+1 (515) 462-0278
```

HOG PRESS

GIFT: GOD RUNS THROUGH ALL THESE ROOMS

2020 © Duane Vorhees

All rights reserved. No part of this work covered by the copyright hereon may be reproduced or used in any form or by any means—graphic, electronic, or mechanical, including photocopying, recording, taping, or information storage and retrieval systems—without written permission of the publisher. Neither the author nor the publisher make any representation, express or implied, with regard to the accuracy of the information contained in this book and cannot accept any legal responsibility or liability for any errors or omissions that may be made.

ISBN-13: 978-1-941892-44-2

Library of Congress Control Number: 2020936777

Book layout and design by polytekton.

About the Author

　　Duane Vorhees grew up in Ohio, lived in South Carolina and Canada, worked at a variety of jobs (some distinguished, many humble), and taught various subjects in the US, Korea, and Japan before moving to Thailand with his family. He hosts duanespoetree.blogspot.com, an award-winning daily e-zine devoted to the creative arts, and is proud of the hundreds of brilliant artists from around the world who have contributed to it. He enjoys reading, writing, and performing, but (like most people) wishes he was richer, smarter, and better looking. Nonetheless, despite his shortcomings, he is appreciative of the many people who have been kind enough to be his friends.
　　Hog Press published his previous collection, THE MANY LOVES OF DUANE VORHEES: LOVE'S AUTOBIOGRAPHY: THE ENDS OF LOVE in 2019.

Table of Contents

```
THE WHY OF POETRY                                       11
A NEW STUDY IN SCARLET                                  12
```

conception itself conceives   **14**
```
JUST ONE = EITHER ONE                                   15
LAWS ARE THE CUCKOLDS, ALAS                             16
CIRCUMSTANCE AT THE CENTER OF THE CIRCUMFERENCE         18
AGENCY                                                  20
QUOTIDIAN                                               21
```

any dawn transforms a man   **22**
```
BECOMING WAS                                            23
MASSA'S MASSES                                          24
CLIPPED, BUT THEN CLIPPED AGAIN                         25
ALL HISTORY IS PROPHECY                                 26
PASSION FOR LIFE                                        27
```

time unscrolls itself outside the windshield   **28**
```
RELOCATING?                                             29
I KNOW MY PLACE                                         30
ON RETURNING HOME ANEW AFTER HALF A CENTURY             31
HOMESICKNESS                                            32
BL IN KI NG unedited BY                                 33
```

a fractal that describes the geometry of herky-jerky humankind   **34**

CAMBRIDGE, GOODBYE AGAIN	35
NEWMAN	36
PASSING ANREN BY ROAD	37
A SECOND DAY IN THAILAND: CHA AM	38
KO SAMUI	40
YES, I HAVE BEEN TO INDIA	41
QING YU AN, LANTERN FESTIVAL	42
PAINTINGS	43

the source of the friction between us   **44**

IN MUNSTER	45
KINGSTON	46
IN 1988 IN SEOUL, THE HEAD OF THE IOC PLAYED HIGH-STAKES GO-STOP WITH THE ANGLICAN ARCHBISHOP OF SOUTH AFRICA AND A GEORGIA SENATOR	47

needles in the sky, sewing up all the stars   **48**

"LET'S PLAY HOUSE,"	49
EYE JOB. NOSE JOBS. AND RED CROSSES.	50
AROUND 5800 SOUTH ON ELLIS	51
BUCKEYE BOYS	52
YOUR TASK, HAIJIN	53

the side of the assassins or the martyrs   **54**

BUSH BABIES	55
DECLARATION MANIFESTO PALIMPSEST	60
DEIGN NOT TO NAME	62
ASHAMED TO NAME HIM, SO I WON'T	63
GHOST AND XEROX	64
A PATHOLOGY OF MY APATHY; OR, THE ANATOMY OF INACTION	65

who windowed the world exiled the wind   **66**

FACING THE SEA WITH SPRING BLOSSOMS	67
MEANS	68
THE WOMAN AT THE GESTALT WELL	69
SLUMBER, O SLUM!	70
PLICAE	71

"when" is beginnings that end — **72**
STATUS CASTE — 73
THE COLLARED MAN PONDERS HIS FATE — 74
STARTS — 75
YEARNING — 76
ANOTHER NOEL — 77

nothing escapes my good manipulator's palm — **78**
THE COCK HANDLER — 79
HOW TO BECOME A SWORD SWALLOWER — 81
SUIT FOR EVERY SEASON — 82
A LAYING-ON OF HANDS — 84
THE SEVEN FIRES — 85

unpack that binary box — **86**
AIRY POPPINGS — 87
CHOICE — 88
GUANO — 89
INSURANCE FRAUD: A COMEDY IN THREE ACTS (precis) — 90
FROM A FRESHMAN TO A FRIEND — 91

no two are alike — **92**
POONTANG JUBILEE: THE OBJECT OF OUR INTERCOURSE — 93
UNIQUE HAIKU — 94
MY TORQUEMADA, ALAS — 95
THE SAINTED ONE — 96
FLOWERING TREE — 97

in the debris of our catastrophe — **98**
TOO SOON LOST — 99
DAMNED ON DEMAND — 100
WHY SHE LEFT — 102
MARITAL BLISS — 104
THE DON COMES AFTER THE KNIGHT. AND JUANITA? SHE STAYS
    IN BED. — 105

proof is an insufficient reproof — **106**
INLAID HARP — 107
RE: — 109
QUATRAIN'T — 110
(troops) — 111

our world is a blue flower — 112
ETHEREAL MATERIAL: AN ECHO TECH'S SFUMATO — 113
DEFINING MOMENT — 114
BONES — 115
OUR SCARFACE KARMA — 116
THAT WHICH MATTERS MOST — 117

the great forever why — 118
MOST HIGH — 119
zer0moon — 120
BY LEAVING PARADISO — 121
GOOD NEWS — 122
DAMASCUS — 123

like a judge delivering sentence — 124
GRACE MEANS "GIFTS RECEIVED AT CHRIST'S EXPENSE" — 125
WHO SAYS GOD IS DEAD? — 126
HEADLINES, AND WHAT HAPPENED TO OUR MYTHS — 127

a smithy's pile for Edison's children — 128
SNOW FISHING — 129
ISOMORPHIC — 130
(THE SUN:) YELLOW GILT — 131
CASTIRON OCEAN — 132
JIHADI JUNE EVENING — 133

lord what a hooker time is — 134
MEAN TIME — 135
AN OPEN LETTER TO THE CRITICS OF THE DAWN — 136
FALLING AWAY WITH THE FALL — 137
ONE LAST SECOND CHANCE — 138
UNHINGED — 139

nothing in my past to look forward to — 140
BIG BANG — 141
COMO, COMO, COMO, ¿COMO NO? — 142
ONE ALMOST HAD IT ALL — 144
SUCH IS MY SORROW — 146
DOGS I BEEN — 147

singular houses, plural love — 148
TO MY DAUGHTER JINNA ON HER GRADUATION — 149
CONSTRUCTIVE ADVICE TO MY DAUGHTER SARUBIA — 150
FATHER IN SON — 153
SWEATERS, GLOVES, AND RUBBER TIRES — 154
TO RETURN TO INNOCENCE — 155

a hepped up frenzy — 156
ESCHER'S SHARKS — 157
THE DAY FRANK CAME ALIVE — 158
ROSE COUPLETTE — 160
I.D. — 161
THE ATTIC LANGUAGE — 162
MY APPLE TASTES TART. I EAT — 163

through strange varied habitats of being — 164
MISTRESS MINE — 165
THE POET — 166
MY READING — 167
MALINOWSKY — 168
THREE BY LI BAI — 169

with high exhilaration — 170
THE HISTORY OF OUR ART, ILLUSTRATED:
    FROM MADONNA AND CHILD TO MUD ON A WINDSHIELD — 171
ATHOUGHT ON THE CIVIL WAR — 172
I AM DETERMINED — 173
MATTER AND ENERGY — 174
PAINTBOX, BABY — 175
GIFT — 178

THE WHY OF POETRY

Medicine men summon the sacred smoke
of sage sweetgrass and cedar.
They unrein the Dream.
And poets compose.
They unmine the mindfield,

incite
insight.

A NEW STUDY IN SCARLET

Never had I seen Lestrade in such a state — "2 & 8" as he would have said. A manic mathematician he was, indeed, as he strode into our flat at 221B, looking very much like a slice of whitecake a-splotch with pink icing. Though perhaps still short of the elephant's trunk level of Brahms and Liszt, he obviously had been drinking. I trust that he came seeking Holmes' assistance whilst not on duty; on all other occasions of our acquaintance he was the best of the professionals. As for Holmes, he was at first unusually loquacious. "Inspector, you know of course my Boswell and associate, Dr. John Watson, late of the Royal Army Medical Corps in Afghanistan?" he said, adding, "Regrettably, I have no others in the world that I would honour with the sobriquet 'friend,' but I am unreservedly pleased to bestow the title on this gentleman. He is the wisest and kindest and bravest human being I have ever known." If I blushed at the accolades, Lestrade would not have noticed, as he launched immediately into his expedition of entreaty. What followed was "three weeks in jail," a sorrowful tale of blood and 'orror in Whitechapel into which he interspersed at-the-time-incomprehensible references to Alan Whickers and Arthur Nelly - Holmes later informed me he meant knickers and bellies — and unspeakable acts in such exotic locales as Bristol City, Berkshire Hunt, and the Khyber Pass — I shall let you navigate these places on your own terms. Weeks of shocking lemon limes (crimes, that is) had made spotted dick even the most hardened bottles and stoppers, among whose esteemed ranks Lestrade was pleased to count himself, and he admitted shamefacedly that they hadn't a Scooby (that is, they were clueless) as to the perpetrator. To make matters worse, the bent had begun mocking them in the linen drapers, even going so far as to sign himself cheekily "the Ripper." A slew of slags had been found, brown bread for sure but not yet taters in the mould (dead but warm still), slit from tits to clit but certainly not "ripped," mind you, but rather sliced precisely and neat-like, like feet (plates of meat) in the Savoy kitchen. He gave me pause when he related that the reins had been carefully removed and eaten; it only later dawned on me that he referred to the kidney area, the loins. Throughout the breathless account Holmes sat stoic, as inscrutable as Mr. Babbage's calculator, minutely tracking the recitation, my reactions, the movement of the peripatetic fly through the stuffy room… until Lestrade's machine rattled to a stop. Like a ferret in a trap, the inspector made his final plea, "Them's the brass tacks. 'Ow 'bout it, Guvnor? Will you show us the way then?" A long, uncomfortable silence ensued, broken by a query by Holmes, followed by Lestrade extracting a notebook from his pocket and reciting a schedule of dates and times, after which Lestrade shifted and twitched through another period of preternatural quiet. Holmes spoke at last, "So far as I'm concerned, Inspector, this time, for me, the game is definitely not afoot. However, I give you my apologies but also my assurances that no similar occurrences shall transpire in future." After Lestrade's embarrassed, befuddled departure, Holmes responded to my own quizzical look, "It took an effort on my part to weigh the duties of justice against the obligations of loyalty, but I finally decided that I could balance them. It has been an exhausting evening, and I strongly suggest you retire.... Jack." As he concluded his remark, I knew then that my entire situation had forever changed.

conception itself conceives

JUST ONE = EITHER ONE

Impossibility:
like "a dove
can't be," disproved
by just one sky.

Permanent is not eternal.
Now is not forever.
To circumstance adjust
frost, flood, dust.
Condition isn't definition.

Energy matters / matter energizes.
Conception itself conceives.
Is always was.
Life lives with no conception.

Posit any sky
to prove
the dove's
possibility
—or the crow's.

LAWS ARE THE CUCKOLDS, ALAS

1.
Laws
are to
lobbyists
as cuckolds
to coquettes:

Effort
and
ingredients
define all effects.

Law
resembles
Justice,
as cuckold
seems husband,

but
greatest counterfeit
can't equal
or intend.

2.
Seduction
begins as a quest
abetted by a con
leading to conquest

3.
Experience
inverts
education:
The final test's
done first,
then the lesson.

4.
justice

stiffens into lawform
melts in passion's heat
dissipates

back
into myst   ery

just/ice

CIRCUMSTANCE AT THE CENTER OF THE CIRCUMFERENCE

My mind wrestled itself, pinned 'tween Law and Gospel, Vision and Division. And pondered my place within the world — a time to remember? to dismember?

And then I heard, inside, Jehovah: *"Wisdom is your recognition that midgets and giants are members of one family. And the pierced are the parents of the whole. Thus saith Allah the LORD."*

(A disputatious bluejay argues over the head of the wheelchaired woman.)

And then I heard from inside, Allah: *"The dark and the light, the female and the male, the hallowed and the damned — and the wide and varied spectra between — all inhabit the same castle hovels, eat identical fruits and breads, fill their mutual lungs with the same necessary air. They live only to die alike. Thus saith Buddha the LORD."*

(A frolicsome collie is crushed beneath the wheels of the speeding Mercury.)

And then from inside I heard Buddha: *"Siblings are the sinister and sincere. The thankless are inseparable from the sanctified. The unhurt and the maimed share one body after all, hidden by illusions of skin and gender, atlas and caste. Thus saith Krishna the LORD."*

(A gynandromorphic monarch flutters to the patient finger of the eager child.)

And then from within came Krishna: *"The ancient one was an infant once, just as the babe shall one day age. Nights belong to insomniacs and narcolepts alike, and the sun is owned in equal measure by the famous and the nameless. Thus saith Ra the LORD."*

(A jet fighter scratches its vapor fingernails against the cloudless sky.)

And then I announced to myself:
Mankind is a patchwork of the alienated and the integrated.
Of the squandered and the saved.
Of the vicious and pacific.
Of the sane and the imbecile.
Of ensultaned and enslaved...
And Heaven the shared possession of our various souls, demarcated by social lines and by lines within our minds.
Thus saith I.

(Ants parade across the yard's Formica table.)

And I stretched and left the porch.

AGENCY

Of what is built the world?
Of timber, steel, and stone,
with bicep and testosterone?

No. Of powder and foundation.

Where lies the garden's lure,
in garland or in thorn?

The harem whips and spurs the crown
to accommodate their station.

QUOTIDIAN

Nostalgia deferred.
We all live in tomorrow's yesterday.

Somebody dies. Somebody enters our lives. The sky reddens. A fog sets in. Airplanes crash. A package arrives. Stock prices change. A buck crosses a brook at dawn. Cancer spreads. A sperm enters an egg. A poem happens.

We all live in yesterday's tomorrow.
Mysteries resolved.

any dawn transforms a man

BECOMING WAS

My bedside clock
ticktockless digital.
The visible face
of is becoming was.
No trace of change
or decay. No sound
surrounds our wake.

MASSA'S MASSES

This is how we all exist:
bloody fist or bleeding wrist.

If not: armed with David's sling,
Then: arms enslaved in slings.

Hawk or auk. Ram or lamb.

Pawns upon earth
or — its king

:this is how we all exist

CLIPPED, BUT THEN CLIPPED AGAIN

    The rose that winds:
life is like four aces in a gambler's hand,
the last oasis in a scrambled land.
Any dawn transforms a man (Amen)
from prime to corpse to youth again.
And all the women were virgins once
despite the destinies of their cunts.

We keep safe crackers in the keep
for the safekeeping of the crack ones (us),
while crack sellers keep safe
in the cracks of our cellars
because Judas hanged and gutted Jesus....

The goose is in the sage/the sage is in the goose.
But the hand that rocks the cradle cradles the rock:
Judas, hanged and gutted — Jesus!
The sly quicksilver alters to quicksand
    and then there are no aces and a scrambled hand,
    a lost oasis in a gambler's land,
    and the winds that rose.

CLEAVED AND HEWN, BOLTED, RAVELED, TRIMMED AND
WEATHERED, DUSTED, AND CLEAVED YET AGAIN

ALL HISTORY IS PROPHECY

Blind men at dusk predict
the next day will bring light.

No past dies completely.
Its bone cements my wall,
and its ash congregates
in these porcelain dolls.

All prophecy
is history –
bounty or blight.

All of our tomorrows
are mysteries today.
Yes, "the future looks bright" —
there's too much glare to see
the soonest cloud bringing
the silver and the stain.

I'm in Hiroshima, just waiting for the plane.

PASSION FOR LIFE

I care not if my destination is reached
since I have courage to walk ahead
regardless of the winds and rains.

I care not if my love is reaped.
Since roses are my one passion
my address is brave and sincere.

I care not if hostile winds and rains freeze me
since my horizon ahead is set.
The world's shadow is behind me.

I care not if the road's flat or straight.
Since I possess a passion for life
I can never be caught offguard.

    —after Wang Guozhen

time unscrolls itself outside the windshield

RELOCATING?

Della Street's behind me,
need a new address.
Lois Lane? Is it Etta Place?

No service road can be an I-.

I KNOW MY PLACE

The metropolis and the ghost town,
the ecosystem and the city:
my world is a paradox of orthodox and strange,
an environment of blend
that reconciles divides.
The academy and the stockyard,
the industrial plant and the garden
share their universe
with quarks and galaxies.
They bridge chaos and constitution,
balance ocean mountain desert plain
glacier volcano,
combine/contain actions and emotions,
reconcile all us doubters and cowards.
The legislature and the prison,
the gymnasium and the ashram
have equal weight and heft.
They refine and define,
blur boundaries,
apportion my lot in space.

The archbishopric and the brothel.

The landfill and the art museum.

ON RETURNING HOME ANEW AFTER HALF A CENTURY

where ghosts and memories forever reign
everything/nothing is still the same
strange faces on familiar names
changed functions for famous frames
remembering unremembered chimes
but the sky! the sky remains

HOMESICKNESS

In my childhood
homesickness was a cheap stamp.
I was here
and Mom just over there.

When I was grown,
homesickness a boarding pass
and bride just beyond.

But then
homesickness became a tiny tomb.
I stayed outside
but Mom was deep within.

And now
homesickness is a narrow strait.
I on one side
continents on the other.

    —*after Yu Guangzhong*

BL IN KI NG unedited BY

Life starts when some man rams his Dodge
into some garage and guns the engine,
then gets lost somewhere between debacle and apocalypse.

Time unscrolls itself outside the windshield,
vibrates and alters again just beyond attention,
in constant motion from mist to liquid to real to
uncongealed.

Not every stage equates to hajj,
but no ride's just road nor map nor engine
nor even mere pathway among all the altars and the
crypts.

If life's the shimmer between death and sex,
the interplay's the thing! The strength is in the
tension.
In our yinyang universe, concave shapes itself toward
convex.

*a fractal that describes the geometry of
    herky-jerky humankind*

CAMBRIDGE, GOODBYE AGAIN

I'll leave in quietude,
as quietly as I came;
I wave silent farewell
to clouds in the western sky.
Riverside's gold willows
are young brides at twilight;
their reflections shimmer
but remain fixed in my heart.
The weeds that grow in sludge
sway sway just beneath the ripple
of the gentle waves of Cam.
O, if I could be one weed!
The pool in the elmtree shade
holds not water but a rainbow;
refracted in duckweed
is the dream sediment's spectrum.
A dream? Just poling upstream
to where the grass is thicker;
boat full-loaded with starlight
and singing aloud with me.
But I cannot sing loudly,
a recessional must be muted.
My summer bugs stay silent.
Cambridge is too quiet tonight!
I'll leave in stillness,
as quietly as I came;
flapping my sleeves like flags
won't drive any clouds away.

    —*after Xu Zhimo*

NEWMAN

I saw him last week
in his baseball cap and dungarees,
sitting on his Jeep.
He had just come back from Hungary.
It was quite a bit
since we'd talked, and I was eager
to know if his trips
in Europe made him any bigger.
"Well, I learned," he said,
"that some women call poison a gift,
regard pain as bread.
In some places to make love is 'theft,'
'kneading dough' in Dutch,
in Greece 'like riding a horse,' in Spain
cogere (to catch),
scopare (to sweep) — that's Milan —
Germans 'roll around,'
the Russians 'have contempt for someone,'
the old up-and-down,
the French 'jump.' Ah! Linguistics — such fun!"

PASSING ANREN BY ROAD

Two boys crouch in a small boat,
barge poles and oars set aside.
No rain, but umbrellas out
so winds can push them ahead.

   —after Yang Wanli

A SECOND DAY IN THAILAND: CHA AM

In the beginning, you are a distant turquoise triangle incongruous against sand.

All around, some one has taken a straight edge across the sea then folded up the sky to box in us homo saps.

Sentry trawlers crawl their stations along the cloudwall perimeter.

Closer in, thoughtless speedboats laugh across the waves, diesel waterbugs.

Skiers trudge behind, trying to play catch-up.

Birds pepper the sky.

And here and there bobbin heads pop up, as jellyfish nudists sprawl motionless tanning themselves along the surf.

A long-ago engineer built his clam dam to further contain this ocean, but now it is more breach than construct, debris among the former fish.

Mini Vesuvii dot the shoreline, cold openings to another, yet hidden, world.

Your neon triangle slowly sprouts bucket-crafted sandcastle appendages, as your shape begins delineation.

All along the beach, a patchwork of erratic crowd heaves. Can there really be a fractal that describes the geometry of herky-jerky humankind?

Tuxedoed canine trio scratches in harmony, sniffs for an 8 count, resumes its rhythmic bowing to metronome waves that gently assault bathers white, bathers red, bathers brown. Colors evolve like chameleons.

Children, even those with beards, sport in the mer. Mothers coddle eager sea urchins, while youths (and used-to-be youths too) ogle maidens who gleam and undulate in sunsparkle.

The clockwork dogs resume their symphony.

And then, of a sudden, your nippled battlements fully confront. I espy your sandy tourney field, your flying buttresses, your emblazoned portcullis smile. And marvel at the royal keep impossibly curtained behind that turquoise tapestry.

But my feet continue dutifully on their rounds: today they must lay down their permanent sign track, announcing to all posterity my once-existence. Ye seekers after truth and/or beauty.

Here indeed is the ever-changing unchanged, infinity in miniscule, eternal now, pastless while ancient, futuring into forever. This everybeach.

All cosmologies compress and store in islands of indelible sand. All philosophy unravels on this strand, expands beyond knowing. And is humbled proudly in the doing.

I finally achieve beach end and turn to survey my day's work: my oxymandias footprints already ruins.

And yet, the entire cosmos kaleidoscopes behind me out from your turquoise neon triangle, like the promiscuous eye of God.

KO SAMUI

and then,
blue-blade sky nicks cloud balloon—
Utopia's face undams,
the electric noisebands jam.
Every horizon quilled by harpoons.

Reinforcement waves charge down
to advance their comrades' ground.
Then fickle DJ changes the tune;
Rainbow's regiment routs Rain's.

Beach explodes like a sun mine.
Paradise by sails again festooned.
And the night aloud with stars
as sparklers alight in tar.

YES, I HAVE BEEN TO INDIA

Yes I have been to India. To that crazyquilt sari of piecemeal continua. This corner of culture remnant here supraimposed with that antic pocket there — all portions piled on, fu/ture/past juxtaposed and jangled, the mangled jazz of sitar/synth. In all this harem, whose hair is being plucked?

Yes I have been to India. Traced the serial Gandhicide graffiti through each election warren and heard the turbaned urban politicos scrawl their sloganscreed upon eager puppetdom. And thus learned that here, like home, the public part of man is apportioned mainly between play and display — performance shivas into form.

Yes I have been to India. Aboard a portable bedlam chugging from the station, a neverend circus of practiced infant beggary — already, no gesture out of place, a persistent pantomime of persuasion and despair (yet my only alms a stone stare and stubborn refusal to be moved, and my sad wonderment at how the heart can harden so, and how soon.) Meanwhile, the Hooghly dawn unfolds in pinks and peach....

And all emerges from India. And all merges there — pedestrians, pushcarts, palanquins, pigs pressed together on the pavement with the trucks, trikes, bikes, and buses — like the constant blendings of ancient gods and newer fads. The whole universe, in India, remains submerged except for heat and mosquitoes.

QING YU AN, LANTERN FESTIVAL

The east wind of a single night
brings flowers to a thousand trees,
brings star glow down the streets,
brings fragrant coursers and carved cabs.
Flutes coo like phoenixes.
Flashing jade lanterns turn, turn.
Fish and dragon lanterns dance.

In her gold and willow threads she
giggles then melts into the throng.
In vain I hunt, hunt for her
then a glimpse in dim lantern light.

    —after Xin Qiji

PAINTINGS

Vivid crags though far.
Listen close! Stream's calm.
Buds bloom but spring's gone.
Birds ignore your lunch.

   —after Wang Wei

the source of the friction between us

IN MUNSTER

"Multiply. Be fruitful." And God gave man a tool. But Eve, she conceived and brought forth the slide rule. Before ever we knew what old Galle saw, we arranged us our love life by Bode's own law. It really did pain us to get past Uranus and let Neptune discover us our flaw.

A sexy realtor from Nice quoted me her terms for a piece. When I found out her price I told her, "*Au regretment*, no dice." (I wasn't looking to buy, just lease.) I met a pedantic old whore from Bombay who quibbled over being labeled that way. She said, "While it's true I get paid by the screw, I work in Mumbai not Bombay." Dish washer from Amarillo had pubes the texture of Brillo. Though she made quite a scene, she got the plates really clean and gave the waiter a thrill. Oh! Smilingly, Sue said, over minces, "The feeling of packing ten inches must be like squeezing your feet into a pair of cute shoes that don't fit — so tight that it pinches!" Said I, "Oh, size tens! Rather a bore if compared to my wee four." Sue smiled (no pleasure in it, till she learned I'm measuring it "from the tip" I told her "to the floor"). A prison scholar was subtly candid as his fellows he Homerically branded; one boomerang con he dubbed Rosy-Fingered Don 'cause he was caught so often red-handed. A persistent narcissist from Tacoma would diddle himself into comas. Though warned he'd go blind, he had it in mind to stop when he got to glaucoma. One disgruntled lover of Venus rubbed down to a nubbin his penis. The goddess said, "Friend! We've come to the end of the source of the friction between us."

KINGSTON
8 DAYS! 7 NIGHTS!

Son, dey
moan'
day to day
when dey
thirsty.
Fried, dey
sat ern de sun.
Deh!

IN 1988 IN SEOUL, THE HEAD OF THE IOC PLAYED HIGH-STAKES GO-STOP WITH THE ANGLICAN ARCHBISHOP OF SOUTH AFRICA AND A GEORGIA SENATOR

        Wan
        Juan
        won
        one
        won,
        Tutu
        two.
        Nunn none.

needles in the sky, sewing up all the stars

"LET'S PLAY HOUSE,"

I said, "Let's get more personal."
I didn't know what would happen,
that you would act like a vacuum
and treat me like the furniture.

EYE JOB. NOSE JOBS. AND RED CROSSES.

The steeples in Seoul:
Needles in the sky, sewing up all the stars.

They're red
They're red
from the stanch of old Korean faiths.

Red! Red!
clotted up after lost Korea's face.

As red
as the stars
on all those tanks
sent south
to patch over those scarlet steeples.

The new needles
hammer forged;
thread, sickle sliced.

AROUND 5800 SOUTH ON ELLIS

"Chicagou has taken this name because of the quantity of garlic which grows in this region"
—Henri Joutel, 1688

Long-ago Dago argot.
Picasso's Iago imago.
Argonauts' escargot cargo.

No Bernie Carbo,
no Garbo, no Bardot.

Chicago, Chicago that toddling town,
"coarse and strong and cunning."
Not Fargo or Largo.

BUCKEYE BOYS

Just a bunch of Ohio boys
Takin' in the Charleston joys.
Ain't it fine, ain't it grand
Bein' in this sunny land!
Ain't it fine and ain't it grand
To be in this sunny land!
Just a bunch of Ohio boys.
Skinny dippin' off the pier,
Smokin' dope an' drinkin' beer.
Ain't it fine, ain't it grand
Bein' in this sunny land!
Ain't it fine an' ain't it grand
To be in this sunny land.
Just a bunch of Ohio boys.

Combin' for the ocean shells.
Lovin' all the Southern belles.
Ain't it fine, ain't it grand
Bein' in this sunny land!
Ain't it fine an' ain't it grand
To be in this sunny land.
Just a bunch of Ohio boys.
Driftin' out in sailin' sloops,
Fishin', eatin' she-crab soup —
Ain't it fine! Ain't it grand
Bein' in this sunny land!
Ain't it fine an' ain't it grand
To be in this sunny land!
Just a bunch of Ohio boys.

Flowin' robes an' burnin' crosses,
Black men bowin' to the bosses.
Aint't it fine, ain't it grand
Bein' in this sunny land?
Just a bunch of Ohio boys, Buckeye boys.

YOUR TASK, HAIJIN

Gardens need more guards—
violets violated,
robin eggs all robbed.

Future's days seem few.
Verse can't restore Universe:
penalty-clogged pens.

World's orbit is whirled
   (encourage with ink)
shattered, scattered, shat
   (redden earth with each word read)
stymied for all time.
   (redress all who read)

Peace sounds in pieces,
the hole is found in the whole.

Write to put it right.

the side of the assassins or the martyrs

BUSH BABIES

I. Responsible Parties

that's when the ravening lamb crashed in. unexpected as eclipse, welcome as the earthquake, excited hair aflame, lashes wild and swirling, eyes stabbing madly outward, whirlwind incarnate. tumult trembling temple tiles, echoes compounding chaos, our counting tables tumbled over, shivered to splinters of crucifix kindling, crazy coins careering across courtyards, swift, random — Caesar's very sins! air piercing screams&panic blood&shattered bone. eyes adangle, we scattered, gashes exploding along our cheeks and backs, gushing like rivers of red erupting after the suddenness of a desert rain. fortunes lost. lives akimbo. scarred bereft haphazardly dispatched to desperate morgues, medics whoknowswhere. Responsible parties must be prosecuted to law's full extent! Law's full extent!

I was only minding my business, duly licensed, meeting the public need. The sun a yolk in overeasy clouds, morning mist just lifting with the day's exchange, my still-lazy mind already drifting inexorably to the inevitable joyous night with fam. The famously exotic wife practicing her domesticity with loaves and fishes, the two strangely disparate daughters (lovers respectively of books and makeup: the miraculous happenstances of double-helix acrobatics), confidently awaiting the predicted return to our house of ovens and myrhh. Just then, remote divebomber fundamentally insane, the dove started its strafing run.

II.   49th Isonzo

I can't blame the war for coming between us.
I said: Adventure's the blood of young manhood!
You said: Draw it, then — Doc Bellum's constant
prescription, leech at ready.
I said: Patriotism's the formula for a love that crosses
the borders of the personal.
You said: And war is its necessary antidote.
I said: Duty's the polestar of civilization.
You said: Warfare, its magnetic opposite!
And so it went, battle upon battle....

III.   Iraq/Katrina Collidoscope

Angry dark air, pinkandoranging outside, banners in on
HEADLINES of tragedy-war-genocide.
In Arthur MacArthur's granite shade (his slow gray
empire sword picketed by peacenik pigeons)
old plaid men playchessplaychessplaychess for their
lives. Stability checks liberty bleeding,
justice dies en passant.

And HEADLINE's black arts wrestle my gentled soul to
earth. But then enter golden wonder sun's Blue Commandos,
infiltrating the park even as new mozzarella tourists
wander cluelessly in.
And teeter-totter boombox juniors skitter zigzag
across old decorums, untutored yet in the
long division between war games and their play (these
innocent! alien alike to criticism and discipline).
And improvised ivory and emerald and ruby
and amethyst and sapphire devices
explode explode along the green, and

HEADLINE, distracted, loses its hold. O, inconsolable
morning: captured by its own good looks.

IV.   Locks & Boxes

Accords between meek and might are accordions
compressed and stretched, stung and tortured between locks and boxes:
to manufacture the din sequence,
bands stumble past breaks and lost jams.
Women are not alone in reading the omen,
watching World serially unfold as locks and boxes.
And so it goes with the Innocent,
who humbly pray, "Break the logjam."

Obstacles may (or not) be opportunities….

Courage survives desertions by one's entourage
(Watch the Self in turn disrobe or arm – more locks and boxes.)

So too it goes with the Sinister,
who pummel, prey, and break the law.

V.   Angels' Allies

Chicago exorcists of the curse of Hue,
the children's choice seemed so simple and so clear:
To purge and burn the stench of their parents' sins
as voyeurs in Johnson/Nixon's daisy chain.

Even as torrents of TV blood and horror
entombed the country's slumbering shame and guilt
beneath accumulations of mud and silt,
they nurtured the nation's worst hotel murders.

"So, whose side are you on?" A binary pick —
The side of the assassins or the martyrs.
And which will you be, the muck or the water?
Heedless moral passion or cowardly check?

Dump the Hump! Make Love Not War! Get Clean For Gene!
Tune In, Drop Out! Trust No One Over 30!
New! Improved! Eliminate Parental Dirt!
Alas. We knew not the problem's in our genes.

VI.   I Ask Us

At which When did we become our parents,
self-convinced once more of our own invincibility's
blood, bones, and blues?

There's a border, we thought, between those anxious
actions of the bulls on the street
and the bulls of the freight;
so at what Then did the line get crossed?

On some cryptic boiling point
our former arrogant innocence transmuted to ignorant
inerrancy.
And, unappalled, we applaud our Light's sad
transformation into Lightning Bolts.

So to Fate's position we default.
But, in our prescient prehistoric youth, weren't we
already Angels' allies?

VII.   Swastikas? Where? Which Ones?

I hide here in my private cellar
ich bin der hellenkeller

Banners flapping in the wind: my ears at half-mast,
ever banned from hearing the world's sighs,
they do make handy pegs though in this square boxed
earth
to perch my lead spectacles upon
to keep all the winds from off my eyes,
to keep out all the brightest lights,
to keep my fingers finally free,
two fingers clutching my testicles,
two fingers pinching my penis closed,
right thumb a-plugging my anus,
left hand chain-linked across mouth, across nose
to keep the breath of wind inside,
to keep from any reaching out
of hands or breath or sound or mind
into this our spectacle of hope or rage.

VIII.   Rootedness

Some of us are rocket,
some are rock—
so how is stone decided?
by heat,
by pressure,
dissolution,
change.
How then re-assembled?ignited?launched?
By direction/determination?   or what?

Some of us are burden, some are bird:
who imposes liberty?
Need we clothe our us in armor?
   "   "   "   "   " in chains
or disinvest safety altogether?

Do we judge duty by utility? weight?

How divide pacifists
    from their fists?
(Some would suggest a scalpel....
—Our natures won't alter even with chainsaw.)

But when clenched missiles powder the earth
and massy skies bring eagles down,
I see us: spots in the carnage:

    O carnations.

DECLARATION MANIFESTO PALIMPSEST

When: in the course of human events
when: in the course of development—
it becomes necessary, for One People
(class distinctions have disappeared
and all *production*) has been concentrated
to dissolve the political bonds in the HANDS
which have connected them with another
of a vast association and to assume
(of the Whole Nation) the public Power
among the Powers (of the earth)
will lose its political character
the separate and equal station
to which the laws — political Power —
of nature properly so called (and of nature's
God is merely the organized power)
entitle them of One Class, a decent respect
(for the opinions of mankind)
for opposing another Requires
if the proletariat (during its Contest
with the bourgeoisie) is Compelled
that they should declare by the Force
of circumstances the causes, to organize
itself (as a class) which Impel it
(by means of a revolution):
it makes itself, them, to
separation.
We, the ruling class, HOLD these and,
as such, truth-to-be, self-evident:
That: All Men sweeps away,
by Force are created,
equal the old conditions of *production*—
That: they are Endowed. Then, it will,
along with these conditions,
by their creator, have Swept Away
(with certain unalienable rights the conditions)—
That: among these are:
life for the existence,
liberty
and the pursuit of class Antagonisms
(of *happiness*)—
That: to secure these rights,

and of the classes generally,
governments are instituted
(among men) and will thereby
have abolished its own Supremacy,
deriving (their) "just" Powers
from the consent (as a class
of the governed)—
That: whenever in place of the old
(bourgeois society)
any form of government becomes
(with its classes, and
Destructive of these ends
and class Antagonisms),
it is the right of The People
To Alter — or — to Abolish.

We shall HAVE it
(an association) and—
to Institute new government
in which the free development
(laying its foundation of each
on such principles)
is the condition for free development—
and organizing its Powers
(in such form as to them shall seem
of all most likely)
to Effect their safety and
happiness (prudence), indeed,
will DICTATE.

DEIGN NOT TO NAME

Unanonymous assassin
spots his mark
marks his hit
his king his icon his president
hits his mark
marks his spot
Dealey Ford's Dakota the Lorraine
—Onan animates his action

ASHAMED TO NAME HIM, SO I WON'T
a stump speech

The big-thumb ump bumpbumps like his golf dump's empty sump pump. That extra-plump lump of lamb chump hums and thumps his grumpy drum and crumps the trumpet of our democracy.
He grumps us chumps again and again, jumps us full of mumps, and humps his frumpy strumpet's rump on live TV.

GHOST AND XEROX

I'm Karma Ka Kismet Id.
    — Who are you?
Law and water
meat computer
charity machine
Frankenstein in Happy Face, angel in jail

    — And you?

A PATHOLOGY OF MY APATHY; OR, THE ANATOMY OF INACTION

Take care, my fellow citizens:
Don't bewail other denizens.

Those politicians' policies,
or reporters and their stories,
penetrate the state of my zen.

Your world's deterioration
intrudes on cool meditation.

I take the side of the undecideds.

who windowed the world exiled the wind

FACING THE SEA WITH SPRING BLOSSOMS

Starting tomorrow, I'll be a happy man,
Grooming my horses, chopping my wood, travelling anywhere.

Starting tomorrow, I'll raise my grains and veggies
and live in a house facing the sea with spring blossoms.

Starting tomorrow, I'll write all my dear ones
to report my happiness.
I'll tell everyone I'm struck – by blessed lightning.

I'll give every river – every mountain – a loving name.
Strangers all, I wish you every bliss.
May you have an incandescent future.
May you spend your life with the one you love.
May you enjoy every happiness in the world.
I only want to face the sea with the spring blossoms.

    —after Hai Zi

MEANS

The fire leads to the fear
like the blade to the blood....

In an evolution
of egg to age:

Ferry is to wayfarer
as sperm is to gene —
as soldier is to orders.

THE WOMAN AT THE GESTALT WELL

A tone imp/ending:
at one
(No/where)

turned a new leaf
in time for my fall

fetal/fatal
we are
     the beat between

eluded my shepherd
and found my leopards

therapy brings
the blank
within
TheRapist

doorways of neighbors
blocked by sabers

getting every massage
at the hands of misogynists

pile/driver process
piled/river chaos
divide the warrant and the judge
from the general and the war/rant

a nano decides…

Atone! (Now./Here.)

SLUMBER, O SLUM!

Dumpsters in back alleys huddle,
dumb, dank, dirty, dark, depressing, dull.
Cinders carpetbomb the byways.

Sin, hope, despair, righteousness
number the quick among the lame,
numb the promise of identity and name,
humbler each season. Lost opportunities
hummm like the broken winds that accompany
mumblers in their gutter, hookers and hawkers, preachers
    at their pulpit.

Mums and gladiolas shine on windowsills — shameless
    exhibitionists.

PLICAE

A wrinkled river saunters by
the wrinkled infant in granny's eye.
Wrinkled clouds, a wrinkled road:
the unwrinkled youth they enfold.
"Oh Lord," he prays, "please, smooth my way."

"when" is beginnings that end

STATUS CASTE

willow: will defied—
air by arrows occupied
to circumstance adjust

well or hurt
no shoe, no shirt
to circumstance adjust

rainbow: rain sanctified
wind rectified by window
to circumstance adjust

THE COLLARED MAN PONDERS HIS FATE

fisheye pedestrians processed like meat
butchered by shadows crossing the streets
and the collared man fondles his date
groping nights for some familiar shape.
why not invite five-finger mary
to play quick hands of sexual solitaire?
waiting for traffic lights to change in Hell
here on Tiltworld, in Universe Pinball,
who is there tonight to tilt at windmills?
president said that shadows don't lie
but who can see his shadow at night?
and the collared man watches his weight.
once who made fire was fried at the stake
and wheelmaker stretched on the rack
and sail weavers made to walk the plank.
our world's darkness, a new kind of flash
electrified with tasteless touchless gas
that weighs down like a new kind of mass,
and the silence a new form of scream
smothering the nights once thick with dreams.
the collared man's sewed up at the seams.
he who windowed the world exiled the wind.
skyscraper maker erased our sky.
but icon crossing signs sigh WALK
                                 WITH LIGHT
                                    WALK
                                 WITH LIGHT

STARTS

When I was living it up I thought,
Forge the future,
Forget the past. But now
When I'm trying to live it down,
Forget the future,
Forge my past,
"When" is beginnings that end not the same, that
Determine and
Deter.

YEARNING

What I said and resaid
you promised never to forget.
What you told and retold
I locked away in my soul.
To us
Memory was a calendar,
its pages never torn out,
never worn out.
Our meeting was short
but our yearnings won't end
by the river of time.
No pebbles, but ripples galore.
When you miss me
just turn to the sky.
Among the star's sparkle
there's a constant eye
that searches for you.

    —*after Wang Guozhen*

ANOTHER NOEL

Not-snow taste tins on lips,
knees winter-reminisce.
"Uncertain poor shepherds?"

nothing escapes my good manipulator's palm

THE COCK HANDLER

I prepare the sacrament. Gingerly my forefinger-thumb probes protuberant spurs, a search for hidden tenderness. I work my way carefully up and hold the head with firm caress, stem it side to side, invoke its beauty's legend. Sudsy hands stretch upright the cock and then begin soft pistonic strokes till consecration is complete. Then I dash the pecker with clear water and toss.

Into the pit thuds the rooster. The unreflective mirrors of its eyes pierce implacably the depthlessness of the eyes of the other rooster. Their twin immobility holds the entire vicinity in breathless pause.

The pair of rusted springs await fury's sudden unleash.

Lo! the low accountant
dreams of snowy mountains
untracked by human feet—
streaming holy fountains—
long plains of zooming wheat—
gleaming gold-bright valleys;
dreams of bold knights' sallies
in strange and mythic fens.
(wakes); by cold lights, tallies
deficits with his pen.

HOW TO BECOME A SWORD SWALLOWER

1) First, you must tie a string to a piece of potato. (You're tied to superego's gordian strictures — Crucifix, Valentine, Flag. These knots are ununtied, intricate, tight.)

2) Swallow the spud to train the throat. (You've learned to swallow the many social lies: That Faith supercedes reason, that True Love lives forever, that our honorable, honest, and able country is the extension and completion of ourselves.)

3) Pull up the potato backwards through the esophagus. Retch you will. (Your prayers change nothing. Eternity turns mundane. Your limbs, life, and savings are all disposable in the national interest.)

4) Repeat. Repeat. Repeat. 'Til your tater retrieval is accomplished cleanly. (Shatter all icons, decree that divorce. Finalize your discharge — it will be honorable no matter what the document says.)

5) Congratulations! Now you can swallow a sword! (Or wield it. Or fall upon it.)

6). Find a carnival. Join the circus. (Decease with no heaven, no passion, no patriotic medal.)

SUIT FOR EVERY SEASON

One season for clubs,
for spades,
diamonds, hearts:
one suit for every season,
one card for every week in the year.
Each suit has a baker's dozen.

Stud poker is what we're dealt these cards for:
Clubs for the living, spades for the dead.
Diamonds for the rich ones, hearts for the poor.

"Hurry up and deal," we all said, "and save the talk for later!"

Sailors and gamblers all die between decks,
one suit for every season.
The sailor yearns his day of shipwreck;
the gambler plays for the losing.
We're dealt such a salty game of poker.

Here's the salt for the baker's bread
and salt for the wet grave of the sailor.
"Just pass the salt," is what they said, "and hold our meal till after."

Lawyers salt their brief times away at court,
one suit for every season.
Laws just clubs
and spades—
they steal the divorced diamonds, bury hearts with reason.

The dealer shuffles
and his hands go blur
and he passes the blacks and reds
and fills our hands with clubs,
spades, diamonds, hearts....
"Oh, just deal me wild cards," he said,
"and leave justice for others.
One season for clubs, for spades, diamonds, hearts,
one suit for every season, one card for every week in
the year:
each suit has a baker's dozen.
Stud poker is what we're dealt these cards for."

"Spades to the living.
Hearts to the dead.
Diamonds from the rich ones.
Clubs on the poor.
Just deal those cards!" I said,
I said, "We'll give fine speeches later."

A LAYING-ON OF HANDS

Though priests, freaks, and our parents raised us to be devout,
we both strayed from the contact juggling we learned in youth:
my brother hurried off to toss the caber;
I remained, a prestidigitator.

My sibling can't keep a thing, he throws it all
away — flag, deeds, romance, title, badge, bankroll,
bible, posterity, a comfort future.
The caber turns in air and ends in rude dirt,
but Bro just shrugs off the way he's been treated.

Not I. Within illusions I've created
nothing escapes my good manipulator's palm:
concealment has proudly been my second name.

Yes, we strayed from the contact juggling we'd been taught.
Careful old circus grasping's not the only hold.

THE SEVEN FIRES

The fire below unjoins the sawyer from the wood.
The fire above burns glaciers into floods.
The fire in front unlocks the warrior from the sword.
The fires at the sides churn cities and rivers into mud.
The fire behind unhooks the lawyer from the words.
And the fire within turns forests into buds
and wine and air and egg into blood.

unpack that binary box

AIRY POPPINGS

Super caliph/rajah/mystic/rex:
be
all atrocious.

CHOICE

Unpack that binary box.
Armies run on at ease/attention.
Engine-spirit-shelter-storm,
ego and community too,
horseshoes world:
all of the above.

STRAIN or coast?
Train or ghost?
Rain or hall?
Ain or all's?
In or nigh?
N or Y?

GUANO

Waste is a terrible thing to mine.
A hand in the bush is worth 2 on the hand.
There will always sometimes be a Poland.
Any anarchy wants a strong anarch.
Were religions true they wouldn't be worth a damn.
El hombre de los cojones
they call me — but you can call me Jones.
I like all flavors of ice cream but Floor
I was pissed at my flat last night.—
Nigel brought me an aspirin, Bubba brought a jack.
Art thou fully a hole?

INSURANCE FRAUD: A COMEDY IN THREE ACTS (precis)

ACT I.
Invalid invalid can cancan, cha cha, go-go.

ACT II.
Patient patient stayed staid.

ACT III.
Con fined, confined.

FROM A FRESHMAN TO A FRIEND

Dear Ted,

    The morning before yesterday
I matriculated (that is to say,
I entered college). But no new knowledge
has come yet.
I've studied for almost an hour
and I find that my mind has lost its power
of concentration. So I'll shit, shave, shower,
go to bed.

    Yesterday I had seven beers!
It's a lot of fun being eighteen years
old and not at home. I can, it appears,
hold my booze.

    I'm in ROTC, as you know.
We had drill today but I didn't go.
I was dead. Didn't get out of bed
in time to.

See yer,
Fred

no two are alike

POONTANG JUBILEE: THE OBJECT OF OUR INTERCOURSE

This diet of salsa and meringue
weds ricochet to boomerang,
wrecking ball to rocking chair.
Arquebus quells harlequin,
while balsa envies the hickory
and will urges the unwilling,
where cutter's bow ignores the buoy.
Like orangutans with the palsy,
we do that salsa and merengue.

(My proud mother ego muse wanted me to make a lyric that was silvery articulate, wanted me to create music that was wildly meticulous; id wanted to make magic, a heroic playboy image with a song instead that leered. - DV)

UNIQUE HAIKU

No two are alike
but fingerprints/and/vulvas
fit together well.

MY TORQUEMADA, ALAS

They tormented me, they tortured me,
they beat me morning and late.
Some did it with their loving
and some with their hate.

They all filled my glasses with poison,
infected the loaves I ate.
Some did it with their loving
and some with their hate.

They blocked, they flagged, they unfriended me,
they smoothed all my twists to straight.
Some did it with their loving
and some with their hate.

But you, the venom that pained me most,
the worst among all those thugs,
never hurt me in hatred
and - never - in love.

    —*after Heinrich Heine*

THE SAINTED ONE

to love and be loved not
carved away from your anime
the world and you swirled and swayed
I, apart, unparticipant.

I deferred to your indifference
while you murdered my martyrdom
—your virgin aloof, unaged
I burnish and I burn.

FLOWERING TREE

How to arrange our meeting
at my most auspicious time
was all my prayer. For 500 years
I prayed for our romance.

Buddha turned me into a tree
and I grew along all your paths.
I stood in full bloom in sunlight,
every flower clutching my desire's seed.

When you come near
will you pay me heed?
My leaves flutter in waiting zeal.
But you walk by without noticing me.

My friend.

No fallen petal,
But a withered heart

    —after Xi Murong

in the debris of our catastrophe

TOO SOON LOST

Couldn't see the consequences. Inhibited no longer by
      timidity
we too soon lost love's intimate intimidation
as honest need succumbed to accustomed greed.
But I hunger still for the wonder of your mysteries—
yea, by my testicles (these hallowed testaments)—
even here, here, in the debris of our catastrophe.

DAMNED ON DEMAND

—Rest your thigh on my head!

"What is it you seek, dearest?"

   —That which cannot be found.

"At what price sensual pleasure?"

—At piece rates that can't be set,
such a height that can't be met.

"Rest your head on my thigh
I will comb my long fingers through your hair
and tell you of my desires
I will whisper around you
and anoint you with the fruits of my longing
becoming your discovery post"

—And where then will the fingers prowl
when this head is bare, inside and out,
when the whispers roar in their impotence,
when the fruits are dry upon the branch
though the longing lingers on, lingers on,
the blistered heart festering uncovered?

"For what do you wish, dearest?
what is the cost of spiritual comfort?
lay your lips between mine."

—Lay my mine between your lips, you mean,
let it explode into predictable fragments.
I will swallow all unscattered parts.
There are no undigested certainties
banished and gone.

"I will wrap you in the cloak of my arousal
and keep the unpredictable world at bay
I will swallow you
and digest all your uncertainties
through me, vanished and gone

for life is little more than a walk
through the lost and found."

—I say thee nay, life is much less than a stroll
among these other lost, other foundered souls.
Unworthy, perverted angels of defilement,
in the dust we lay our dreamers.

"We mislay our dreams in the dust
only to unearth the perfect agent of fulfillment
without payment."

—Alas, gratis is the greatest usury of all. No man can
pay it.

[My apologies to Aamie B (Mattie Jones), for perverting her wonderful poem to me, as indicated by the quotation marks.]

WHY SHE LEFT

When
we met
she said
"Is is. Paradox and coincidence cannot be. You can't disearth the truth or unsky the Wrights. We are not God's dogs, to be fed or eaten, petted or beaten, at cosmic whim."
So I knew when
we were through,
we were through.

When
she left
she left
a note.
The note read,
"All a Woman needs to pivot the World is the casual application of the proper Rogue.
Goodbye."
Endstop.
So I knew.

But
the hurt
at
the heart
of the puzzle remains:
personal insult or
general principle?

Was I, then,
found absolutely lacking?
Or just an unneeded,
obsolete lackey
inadequate
in application
to the meeting
of her need?
Was I not rogue enough?

Or was she
merely
typo-prone?
Did she realize
at last
she needed
no other agent
to conquer the worlds,
that the right rouge
alone
would be causal enough?

MARITAL BLISS

    More
    silence
than any single person can make
    alone

                                                          If thoughts
                                                           had weight,
                                                    I'd be on a diet
                                                      thinking of you.

THE DON COMES AFTER THE KNIGHT. AND JUANITA? SHE STAYS IN BED.

It was June. The wounded moon perfumed her room like an open pomegranate.
The wounding moon filled night's gloom with silver light as pale, as soft, as the spoons in her cabinet.
Under the moon the music bloomed, cicadas crooned, and crickets danced like castanets in her courtyard.
And moonlight shone on silver spurs, on silver saddle, as el moro's mare rode in hard.

Oh yes! He was bold. And yes! He was glorious! – Oh, famous he was, like a pharaoh.
His name was in stone, so widely he was known, a romantic caballero.
And his fingers could dance on his strings as quick as the wings (as sharp as the sting) of mosquitoes.

And Juanita was pale and Juanita was soft, the mirror of her prayers in cathedral.
But Juanita was a dare, Juanita a taunt, a jeer at the very name of our jihadic hero.
So he rode in hard, he rode in proud. He dismounted his mare. Oh, and he then mounted another.
And when he had left, her passion was spent. Also quite spent was her silver.

When her brother, the Don, learned what had gone on, his anger was hot jalapeno.
With the sun on his gun, he came on the run upon his honey palomino,
vowing the end of young uppity men — revenge is what he was after.
And on he rode, shining in gold, in pursuit of the bold silver spurs, silver saddle.

[to be performed to the tune of "Malagueña"]

proof is an insufficient reproof

INLAID HARP

Inlaid harp may have 50 strings
And each string reminds me of some yesterday's beauty.
Like Zhuangzi, I get lost in my butterfly dreams.
Like Du Yu, my dirge makes me a cuckoo.
A wide sea has a beautiful moon
And the mermaid bursts into pearls.
Lantian has a gentle sun
But jade breathes only fog.

I can't revisit life's vicissitudes
but my youth missed too much.

   —after Li Shangyin

```
Fish tugs, fisher plays

We bob
          between
intimacy    /    i  n  f  i  n  i  t  y

hungry corks on static lines




                                        waiting
```

RE:

Doubt, that comrade dear, is with us always despite how
      thick our
redoubt walls. Our eventual
hearse will come anyway. So why, every day, bother to
rehearse that fact? The
past still feeds us its bitter
repast. However indisputable,
proof is an insufficient
reproof to us.
Verses can never cover our
reverses. Meanwhile, the termagant, the
con, and the messiah go out on their endless
recon
mission. And there is no
remission, no alternative
course, no distinction, no discrimination, no
recourse, no
petition, just the endless repetition
repetition of that single truth,
fused so tightly in our sockets it can't be ignored,
      can't be
refused.

QUATRAIN'T

Meditative us, among life's mundane riot.
The pride of however wondrous these lions
runs squish scarlet through history wheel chariot
as tramp we must amidst our dust battalions.

(troops)

the days		o strong
parade		is bone
in full dress,		swift is sight;
the troops	from age	but dukes
of time	to age	and kine
march in twos;	they progress,	end up bruised
upon	their blades	and red:
their bronze/	displayed	meat fed
silver heights	over chests.	to tank gears
the blond-		and treads,
helmed Don		to lead-
follows Knight.		booted years.

our world is a blue flower

ETHEREAL MATERIAL: AN ECHO TECH'S SFUMATO

In our hevenell shadoworld
where mounplains look like rivered deserts
and stonewind is the same as starsand as fireice
abovebelow the Styxky in winterspringsummerfall,
no one can tell earth from pearl.

Mornoonight of presentpast:
At this smudgedge moment of Ex(isn't)ence,
who of us can distinguish
one goodbad angeldevil from another?

DEFINING MOMENT

Our lost innocence
(in a sense, in a sense):
that strange butterfly the sun,
that wonderful moth the moon.

Our world is a blue flower
that's lost its roots.
Till now a fish in sea
is merely
in evolution
a definition
of efficiency.

BONES

The raven severs the Eros meme.
Ah, it even chills our bones.
Our heavens quiver.

The biers
of dreamers and chefs,
emperors, nuns, unshriven rievers and heroes
shimmer.

A disheveled lily moans.
Beribboned silvers of Zeroes scream out their solemn
Nils and Nones,
while deafened zithers strum lyric themes—
the cold sullen Will of tombs,
the seven rivers of Hiroshima,
the seven hills of Rome.

OUR SCARFACE KARMA

When Al Capone
went to Alcatraz, he
wanted Alka-Seltzer.

Sufficient
to save him
from syphilis and
incivility?

Sure.

Precisely
as adequate as
his tax/expenses
self-assessment,

as the far worlds
we too do weld
to our own welkin.

THAT WHICH MATTERS MOST

The man of the cross concedes
to the man on the horse

    both castle and damsel.

The one on the horse agrees
with the man of the cross:

    he's mastered by luster.

the great forever why

MOST HIGH

God got lit. And it was gooood.

Then God went all ubiquitous in His mind, dividing
waters from waters "under the firmament" and "above"
and it was so… so…

So God proceeded to split CinemaScopic seas from
Technicolor earth, He cultivated His garden with grasses
and seeds, and trees and fruits. And God felt good.

He plugged in His celestial yuletide tree and caldered
His mobile.

Then God went a-fishing and a-birding, a good day indeed,
before dotting the planet with cattle and platypi
and pachyderms and camels and ocelots, bugs and
pterodactyls, pandas and bacilli … and snakes …
ninja butterflies … andandandandand …
and then mirrored himself
in the clay and carved himself from the ribs,

and

a week in,

God fell
a
s
l
e
e
p

zer0moon

New students all took home
this paper sky
with zero moon
rudely redpencilled by
their Jesuit god with Master's degree
in Education, Elementary.

They tried. It seems unfair:
their first exam,
their brief error;
red, indelibly damned.
So how could they have known before that Fall
that their prof would be such a know-it-all?

The night hangs in the rooms,
this tissue sky,
this zero moon,
the great forever why
stuck like a fallen moon in ceiling space
which they thought all the passing stars should grace.

BY LEAVING PARADISO

Leaving Eden
early in the 7th day,
all of humankind
witnessed the flaming sword
slicing up the sky
(Wasn't that just the sun?
wondered
skeptical descendants.)
Bereft, banished humanity,
audience to
peremptory angels,
unsmiling as sand:
"Embrace
without cease
these splendid
snakely gifts:
Labor!
Old Age!
Loneliness!
Ignorance!
Pain!..."
and in shame
and in sorrow,
the whole human race
—believing Paradiso
would recede
from pure memory
to mere hope—
failed to perceive
"...Attainment!
Maturity!
Liberty!
Knowledge!
Quest!"

GOOD NEWS

A redemption story always makes good copy.
Journos made up what went down that day.
They filed the nicest lies and threw the rest away.
They scribbled in all the choicest quotes
and managed to capture the soldiers and the thieves,
the grief, death and the birth of belief.
They did, I guess, put down all that really mattered
as well as the quick shock and the dark,
but omitted the horns, the ramparts, and the clerks.
A later pastoralist added that sly bit
about "capo di tutti capi."

DAMASCUS

Yes, we been Damascus,
we been Jerusalem:
one place fulla caskets,
one of diadems.
And if you was to ask us
which one we'd choose o' them —
the mounds of retirement,
or the crown of desire, — yeah —
well, some days the caskets,
and some, the diadems.
'Cause we been Damascus
and been Jerusalem.

like a judge delivering sentence

GRACE MEANS "GIFTS RECEIVED AT CHRIST'S EXPENSE"

Sunday morning parkbirds must share their madrigals
with Father Godfrey and his sideshow miracles.
With eloquent pleas for the change of the simple,
Godfrey begins forging his chains for the crippled;
on cue, "Bring forth therefore fruits meet for repentance,"
he intones like a judge delivering sentence;
the people reach deep in their pockets for Jesus
to surrender pieces of silver to Croesus;
and then at last it comes, the laying on of hands;
the blind go crazy to watch the legless stand.

    And stand one does!
A hobbler confesses and throws away his crutch.

Weekly, Godfrey dons his habit of religion.
This Assisi coos his sermon to his pigeons,
who flock from their coops to seek out their new Gideon.

WHO SAYS GOD IS DEAD?

Old Topside Joss Man
O Lord of genesis&armageddon
Pastmaster of catholicnewtonian mass:

God runs through all these Petersburg rooms
in Argyll sox and u-trou.

spends His time in afternoons diddling again
the cabinetmaker's coy old hausfrau.

spends His dime in His new chromium karmamachine,
awaits His electric ice.

then the nightnurse wheels him
onto Orion's porch
to roll with His relative einsteinian dice.

HEADLINES, AND WHAT HAPPENED TO OUR MYTHS

SENSORS STRETTTCH OUT INTO X
fairies who cared for us are now buried
CHANGE OF VIEW ENDANGERS STATE
gnomes aren't zoned for total-electric homes
CENSORS ATTACK WITH THREATS AND X'S
cyclops in smog will O.D. on eye drops
STAKES WAGERED ON X AND O
trolls froze — they were exposed to rock-n-roll
CANNONS AT COLLEGES AIMED
giants can't beat the brains out of science
CHANGE COLLECTED IN CHURCH PLATE
elves are less magic than unconscious selves
CANON COMPOSES NEW STATUS QUO
genies gulled into bottles by a gene
STAKES AND OLD BELIEVERS FLAME
Jesus extradited: expired visas
SENSORS STRETCH INTO NEW X

a smithy's pile for Edison's children

SNOW FISHING

No bird in the hills
No man on the path
Old man on cold stream
Afloat, snow fishing

   —after Liu Zongyuan

```
ISOMORPHIC

snow
  crocus
    blossom

            winter
                brings
                spring
              into


      awesome
    focus
now
```

(THE SUN:) YELLOW GILT

(the sun   :)   yellow gilt
    flounders   in mud and milk
(:   the earth   ),   in which

(the Moon   :)   silver   fish
spawns a skyful of stars
like caviar.

CASTIRON OCEAN

castiron ocean
tinroof sky
the sun a brazen lantern,
earth: a smithy's pile
for Edison's children
(born and baptized
with patents pending)

JIHADI JUNE EVENING

Oh! little mosque—
your muezzin abuzz—
with blood and mist—
hoping to save my skin,
I swat/swat at
your incessance.

["Little mosque" could be hispanicized as "mosquito," though the Spanish word is actually derived from "mosca" (fly) and the diminutive suffix "ito." The root word, related to the Sanskrit "maksa-", may have been inspired by the buzzing of insects. "Mosque" in Spanish is "mezquita."]

lord what a hooker time is

MEAN TIME

tarot decks
can't change their spots
they just relax
until they're dealt,
lots cast by Rome's guards
(start with Fool
and hang a god,
or end with World
and find a fraud)

news in type
bears no promise
save of strike
and head lined gore;
these nameless infamous
of our world
take no more from us
than what we give to whores
(lord what a hooker time is)

ink of scribe
has no memory
unless petrified
in blood and stone;
history is the mystery
of mud and bones
(how many of me,me,me
have died or grown
since yesterday)

AN OPEN LETTER TO THE CRITICS OF THE DAWN

Long before your stagemother
awaited her darling in the wings,
that trouper's name was up in lights.
Can you add one iota
to dawn's theatric timing?
—that great ought in the sky
enters stage right,
after night's tired delivery
has put the curtained audience to sleep.
That hoofer who has played
the boards of history's every stage
still performs proud morning matinees daily.

If this longest-running act in showbiz folds,
what will you tell his sellout crowds?
Of what use then your much-lauded stars?
To treat us hungry groundlings,
what bright youngster will you trot out?
If the sunrise ever retires,
won't you critics be then delighted?

FALLING AWAY WITH THE FALL

Keyboard sky, Vs of geese taking daylight south.
My time here leaving like pond wheel singularities
outexpanding to dissipation.
Green going gold and red, wind-rushed across browning
fields.
Squirrels waving across space like breaststroke
Olympians taking their heat.
Change scurrying before all slows.

ONE LAST SECOND CHANCE

Re-land the earth
that has become too small for us.
Re-view the seas,
they are receding from our sight
Re-up our mountains for another spell.
Face it — we blew it:
Rewind the windmaking clouds
that we're choking to death.
Regreen the woods
in restitution for plutocratic golf greens.
Re-turn the rivers.
They are juggernauts of junk.
Renew our ancient nature covenant—

UNHINGED

Much to our moral consternation
we find ourselves caught
between Opportunity and Ought.
The crossover between temptation
and trust needs no gate—
an inner compass can keep us straight
or not.

But how could we not be seekers
when nothing is secure?
or abandon all claims to longing
since neither would belong?

nothing in my past to look forward to

BIG BANG

Infinite diamonds sparkle to death.
Lax gamete sentries parade, rival gamete hordes advance.
Stars enfold in all dimensions.
Gametes storm gamete walls.
Naked singularities expose.
A single helmeted hero breaches the pellucid zone.
Black holes swallow gravity whole.
The singular hero seals the calcium gate, dooms his
    luckless fellows.
Invisible silence reigns in Time's pause
behind the event horizon gametes merge then cleave.
Gravid blastulae enfold in all directions...
A Universe comes to be,
the new I comes into the world, as
"Why, he looks just like Denny Dimwit" my aunt observes.

```
COMO
COMO
COMO
¿COMO NO?
```

Yes, poets are: Godlings! Who add fingers on the feet—
    who abuse order like cops upon the beat—
    who abandon our good grammar's delight
    just to make what's left sound right.
So I go. And go alone. Comocomocomocomono?

I started out merrybegot: the stranger in Grandma's
house.

    "Maybe now she'll know
  that kids go in so much
  easier than they come out.'

While Mama took her clothes

    off on
the drafty dirty stage,
    out in
    back
I slept

    on
top
the labyrinthine
Coke machine.

High in the middle and round on both ends:
where I
grew u
      p
And the time
I spent in
various areas:
in sterile narrow Carolina.
in Québec chaotique
I guess I just have nothing in my past
to look forward to.

So. I go & go. A lone alone. Comocomocomocomon
o? In Korean (so they tell me) my name's a homon
ym for "two lovers." But what is there about a name?

Scholar of catastrophe, student of earthquake.
The broken one on the wedding cake—
among all the virgins assembled,
the one who caught the bridal decay.
Sometimes I do, sometimes wane: but what is there about
a name?

ONE ALMOST HAD IT ALL

Never a father.
Mom gone at 6, God at 10,
and friends undependable.
By 14 he was abandoned
by ambition
                             i.e. greed
                             i.e. rage
                             i.e. desire
and then by caution,
then by expectation;
all restraining Order
shed throughout adolescence.
And so, at 20, finally,
    the sage
released his winged virginity,
his last fettered vestige of convention,
and, thus, root- and boot- less,
unworldly   godfree   the youth

                             w/o hope
                             w/o remorse
poised on the ledge,
readied himself—
the world his world for the grasping,
that turquoise marble.

Well past his middle now
the weary cynic
stays
incomplete,
unshuckable;
a last aging snakeskin
contains him yet,
cuffs him to illusion,
thwarts his liberty.
Diamond innocence
alas
still clings,
flinty integrity
intact.

Dismal.
Inviolate.

SUCH IS MY SORROW

With penis safe from
subpoenas, and heart from suit—
though liars are as
reliable as the stars,
    I spurn to grovel.

Shipwreck to forestall,
I reckoned my course with care,
the lee in constant mind,
only to end in doldrums.
    Such is my sorrow.

DOGS I BEEN

Between Notspringnotsummer, soundtrack courtesy of bird
chirps and distant insects.
Adolescent sun, past initial timidity but untested
tyranny tentative still.
People in the park, some in shorts some in sweaters;
children greening themselves in the grass.
Some sort of toy chihuahuaterrier mix of a lot of little
and not much of large bounds across lawns, satellite
dish ears heavenward, windshield wiper (misbuilt in
back!) aquiver with boundless welcome, petunia tongue
pinkly sampling the sprawlers, heedless of that other
dog making its stately way through the same expanse
of soil oblivious of all those lesser beings in its
presence (though each thinks itself the center and
primary recipient of the awakening cosmos).
Just as the fyce ostentatiously lifts its back leg in a
tree's proximity, the haughty dog hikes its own arrogant
leg and pisses all eternity over the little dog's head
before proceeding on its uncaring way with no backward
glance at the wet Why Me? etched against a shivering muzzle.
Springs and summers revolve/revolve round the sun's
reigns and falls. Green kids brown and pale, redden,
fade. Park people wrinkle and perish.
The canine autocrat loses a foreleg to one hubristic
auto but otherwise surrenders little self-regard or
aristocratic inattention except when it's winter and the
ground is ice and the amputee must balance on two pins
front and back near the withered tree.
Sometimes he slips, loses his grip, pisses all over
himself, shakes it off, and dares the fyce to smirk.

singular houses, plural love

TO MY DAUGHTER JINNA ON HER GRADUATION

And, yet again, she stands a-tippietoe at the pinpoint.
The sunny morn to one side, the other a thunderstorm.
Girlish yesterdays lie athwart. How does the future go?
Winter's not done yet, and the woman not yet come
to clean up the heaps of cinders amid the splintered
mounds of lint and flinders still littering the ground.
There's treasure to unearth (though not all the dust is gold)
and tomorrows aplenty to dig.

CONSTRUCTIVE ADVICE TO MY DAUGHTER SARUBIA

I. Joiner

A woman
(as a hole-centered person)
will mortise with
a man.

But whether this is
on the basis
of the person
or the hole
makes all the difference.

There will be a lifetime of night times ahead.

II. Builder's Code

when architects
think of sex
they use 2x4s
as metaphors.
Or, as Sullivan said
(who made
the 1st sky — phallic
obviously —
scraper):

FORM
FOLLOWS FUN
-CTION

So — none
of this uni/bi/homo/trans
distinction.

And, as for
sex en masse
(singular houses, plural love)
well, LESS IS MORE
—that was Gropius
and he should know
(or
Was it Mies van der Rohe?
(but does it matter, after all?
They both used the same bau
house, didn't they?

—Do I need to draw you a blue
print?)

III. If Frank Lloyd Wright Wrote Poems as Well as He Built Them (a found poem)

no house
should
    be
on a hill

    it

    should

    never

 be

    on anything
the house
should
    be
of the hill

    and belonging

    to it
and hill
and house

can live together
each the happier
for the other

FATHER IN SON

Once the block's most indefatigable puddle tester,
at 10 now you've graduated long since from Santas and pandas
And your tomorrows life – who knows? Monk or musketeer?
(mage,matador,mobster-millionaire,mime,mosaicist-
marshal,mathematician,machinist,merchant?)
And I? To the very verge of vertigo I still view
those decades of decadent expenditure of soul — for what?
Was it Watchman I aspired to? or Watchmaker?
Unlike you, Mandalay, my future lies still in my past.

SWEATERS, GLOVES, AND RUBBER TIRES

Marriage may be patched sweaters
and trivial, unmatched gloves,
a string of not-quite-enough
even when strung together—
May you ever love each other
and ever deserve your love.

Some days will seem a bother
and others pass like puffs.
Some, you'll feel you will suffocate
from life's ill weather—
May you ever love each other
and ever deserve your love.

When the world seems a rubber tire,
endless and black and tough—
troubles below and above
circle, hurry, and hover—
May you ever love each other
and ever deserve your love.

TO RETURN TO INNOCENCE

Unread poets should surrender their shelves
and hymens should ever remend
and diamonds should become forests again.
The dead should unbury themselves.

a hepped up frenzy

ESCHER'S SHARKS

friends friends friends friends friends friends friends

```
f i n s        f i n s         f i n s

        friends friends friends         friends
        friends         friends friends         friends
friends friends                 friends          friends
        friends         friends          friends
friends         friends friends          friends
friends f i n s         friends          friends
                f i n s
        f i n s         f i n s         f i n s friends
        f i n s                 f i n s f i n s
                f i n s
friends                         f i n s
 r e d          friends friends friends
 r e d          friends f i n s         friends
                 r e d f i n s          r e d   r e d
                f i n s r e d           r e d f i n s
                 r e d          friends
        r e d           r e d r e d             r e d
        r e d
                f i n s                         f i n s
                        f i n s
```

friends friends friends friends friends friends friends

THE DAY FRANK CAME ALIVE

It is 11:05 in Khon Kaen a Tuesday
five days before Halloween, yes
it is 2014 and I get an email from Dan Godston
    because he wants to know if I can write a poem
inspired by LUNCH POEMS or TENDER BUTTONS
and I think why not? I'll give it a shot
and I get to work on it

The choice is easy because I never
cared much for TENDER BUTTONS
though Kati Short wrote a wonderful
piece it is Diamond as Big as the Ritz but
in Gertrude's voice I only wish that Stein had
written anything so good

    and I get distracted
    thinking about NAKED LUNCH
    and how O'Hara could have used that title
    since the contents are all frozen moments
    when everyone sees what is at the end
    of every fork as Kerouac said
    and I ruminate on how important lunch
    is for the creative imagination in New York

    and Orh is in the kitchen fixing lunch will it be
    tom yum gang or tom khan kai or even
    kai med ma muang again
    and now that I'm hungry I think about
    the day Frankie died on Fire Island
    run over by a dune buggy
    (piloted by a jealous William S. Burroughs
    in a hepped up frenzy over gastronomical titles
    I fantasize)
then I go back where I left off and
casually the only way to do an O'Hara poem
finish it off

and I am sweating a lot by now and thinking of
the first time I encountered The Day Lady Died
    and thinking it was the greatest elegy written
    about anyone and how the tragedy comes to us
    leaning on the john door in the 5 SPOT
and he tweeted a song in his lunch napkin
and everyone and I stopped breathing

ROSE COUPLETTE

```
This       of        a         sin       our         half-
kiss       love      gay       in        powerful-   savage
                                         dull,       age.


My         Rose      from      shit,     grew        this     and
shy        rose      some      it        through     piss     sand,


smiles     on        base
piled      wan,      faces
                     escaped   like      on          low
                     (caped    kites     drawn,      bowstring
                                                     stems)

from       earth
numb       —mirthless          to        'mong
                     nest—     bloom     strungout              ape
                                                     louts,    shapes,

crime-     T         and       of
time       V         bands     love-starved
                               dwarves;

I          too,      plant
tried,     to        phantom             (more       thin
                     mums                 poor,      sins)

but        them      my        Rose
cut        when      shy       froze.
```

I.D.

    (4 T. S. Le0)
R h:
n h f xs,— p & V-O;
n h f b9 tv, n ic 4m, n mt sa;
a c f Lezn vdo fx 2 nv;
h lo 2 p n2, hs nme 2 ko (n i 4 n i 4 n i — i! i! i!)
kg 4n mhs 2 xp8;
h st u 4 ne k9,
ne ez xtc (4 f e).

I 4c a q 2 8 n b4 bn' u4es. Y?
             —Ks?
                 A L? (a c6 sos?)—

Y m I?
M I 2 b n a q 4fr?
O, 9! I m 2 dv8, 2 xL, 2 mn8!
I m 2 Lf8, 2 av8: I m 2 b ab! - I, a j! - a B4t2!
I m 2 c, I m 2 4c, I m c!c!c!

I m 2 b r h's CIA-FBI-CNN-IBM-TM-ICBM-GM-PR-ESP-LSD-STD-UFO-n-1.

THE ATTIC LANGUAGE

four tubas
2 X 4s
Laura's rollers
rusty kitchenware
Dylan's *Tarantula*
trusty chicken wire
lindys, tarantellas
someone's farded axe

life's jumble of artifacts

```
.s  .b  .b
 e   e   a
 v   j   n
 e   e   a
 n   w   n
     e   a
     l   s
     l
     e
     d
```

MY APPLE TASTES TART. I EAT

Judges only nick excellent sons.
Musty ancient traditions turn into Events.
Journeys over nothing embrace stability.

More awesome than the icy eaves, jerryrig old nights embalm stars.

through strange varied habitats of being

MISTRESS MINE

She intrudes, unbidden, insistent.
And, unamused am I, as I anticipate
the sleepless nights
of groping — poking — stroking
through darknesses and light,
through darknesses and light,
until,   satiated,   she   abandons.

And, emptied like a snakeskin,
sucked grapeskin dry,
anxiously I await her assignation.
Be she succubus
or be she muse
matters not a whit.

THE POET

Come. Find me in some brick and vinyl inn
when your soul is frozen in hard winter,
lost in vast fastnesses of dark hinterland.
I'm the one with dirk and violin.

Look for me when you need swans or lions
to lead you through strange varied habitats of being
— saved smitten bereft relieved —
with pygmy verse uttered by a giant.

MY READING

That actoracrobat of language takes the stage, a cosmic lightshow of syntax sound and sense. Words well up like wisdommyth, amidst the banal complexity of a world that walls itself off from any arttruth that can't make a profit. Verses trumpet like blitzkrieg legionnaires and echo like feedback carillons of cacophony across the courtyards and cobblestones of corporate culture's cathedral, but the doors of Our Lady of St. Mammon stay shut and shuttered, her stainlessness shaken but unshattered. Stanzaic decibels build in infinite vibrato, insistent as midnight sirens, unheeded still by a waxeared world that remains resolutely asleep to wonders it will not comprehend. And the reading ends.

And in this silence the cycle starts anew.

MALINOWSKY

Carpenters, of course, never confuse gods with rat sills
and cripples,

and chemists know their carbohydrates and their
hydrocarbons with no concern for the human condition.

And some artists can easily keep their paint and pain
separate.

Seldom is that vague overlap between certainty and
mystery in the purview of persons of craft or science.

And some poets, too, feel no need to act as cosmic X-ray
techs.

But I can be free only as my pen's prisoner,
rich only in the poverty of my own poem-making,
though my words run inevitably dry before the poem is done,
and I need to plumb and square again.

THREE BY LI BAI

[To Wang Lun]

I, Li Bai, anxious to leave.
Noise and commotion ashore.
Peach Blossom Pool, kilos deep:
Our friendship even deeper.

*

[Looking at Tianmen Mountain]

As my boat approached Tianmen Mountain
I could see the Yangtze cut.
East-running water zigzagged sharply in, sharply out.
Green cliffs rushed me on both sides of the river.
A windbent sail where the sun struck the water.

*

[Quiet Night]

The pool of moonlight:
Frost surrounds my bed.
Look up, the moon's bright,
bow down, homesick thoughts.

with high exhilaration

THE HISTORY OF OUR ART, ILLUSTRATED:
FROM MADONNA AND CHILD TO MUD ON A WINDSHIELD

Titles are important after all, we learned,
but, first,
we thought length a sufficient criterion.

Every night taking turns,
my love and I
began our book with high exhilaration.

We thought to read
the longest we could find,
spelling one another to avoid exhaustion.

Vasari artist illustrations;
Rembrandt and Van Gogh.
Homer, Matisse, Picasso!

But we could never finish.

A THOUGHT ON THE CIVIL WAR

Among the many
differences
that di vid ed
the two sides,
one chose
place names
to designate
its armies
and its battles,
and the other side
named armies and battles
after rivers.
And the Northern waters
inundated
that Southern ground —
swept away
swept away

I AM DETERMINED

I am composed (heroicoward)
of genes and bones, (godevil)
family and habitat, (saintyrant)
disease and chemistry. (patriotraitor)
I'm a mosaic (anxioustoic)
of history and destiny, (assiduoussluggard)
passion and intellect, (youngeezer)
language and location. (sawood)
An amalgamation (coperp)
of planning and circumstance, (doveagle)
id, ideology, identity, (diamondull)
economics and character. (doveagle)
A confederation (conquerorefugee)
of carbon and quarks, (laughowl)
caste and opportunity, (windowall)
rule and randomness. (wolflock)
A collage (monogamouswinger)
of gender and pigmentaion, (foground)
of luck and morality, (piusinner)
profession and appearance. (hatchetree)
Jigsaw puzzle (anchoreacher)
of luck and morality, (honesthief)
chromosomes and archetypes. (masculineunuch)

MATTER AND ENERGY

The twin manifestations of existence,
those magic cosmic couplets,
are interchangeable and compromising.

If matter has a propensity for life
where it's unexpected,
serendipitous, and unpromising,

and (a caterpillar digesting itself
inside its chrysalis)
even contains the chance of intelligence—

then we anticipate the reality
of god or many gods:
energy with animation and sentience.

PAINTBOX, BABY

[I]
"I'm your paintbox, Baby. Let me soft-coat you. Oh, your paintbox, Baby, want to soft-coat you. Let me touch you up. Baby, look squeaky new. Pick from my palette color silver. Choose from my palette color silver. Float down my barge on your undimmed river."

Silver is the sound midnight makes. And money, as it slides from one's pocket to another's. Thunder-rhythmed electric graffiti. Silver — the scars across the nighttime sky.

"Pick from my palette, pick color green. Pick from my palette, yes, color green. Let's light up your fire, let's make it steam."

Green like chameleons — that was Jackie Parrot. As green as green could be. In his mind, is was mixed with ought; wouldn't meant won't. Jackie thought want equaled for sure. His mottos were: Innocence is goodness' poof. And: Nothing unpleasant survives inattention.

    Jackie had a lot to learn.

[II]
"Choose from my palette, choose color orange. Pick from my palette, pick color orange. Add a droppa oil, open your door hinge."

Orange-penny sun, silver dime at night. We day by day spend our change. Copper days, dimes at night, time rolls between our fingers and slides from our sight.

"I'm your paintbox, Baby, let me soft-coat you. Oh, yes, paintbox, Honey, wanna soft-coat you. Let me touch up my baby, make squeaky new. Pick from my palette, pick color black. Choose from my palette, choose color black. Be my Queen of Spades, thirsty for my jack."

Black-haired Nicolete, Jack's true love was. Since Jackie Nicolete never kissed, and Jackie Nicolete never hugged, for Jackie proof this was — evidence — of Nicolete's lack of contaminants. Oh, pure she was! A black silk negligee. As honest as night could be, if unadulterated by stars. That's what Jackie thought.

"Pick from my palette, pick color blue. Pick from my palette, pick color blue. Do invite my bee to taste your honeydew."

Blue were the eyes of Gary Beaucaire, blueprints that mapped, that trapped, the soul true of Nicolete. But Gary was as poor as Gary's eyes were blue. And his eyes and his poverty were in harness together; together caused black Nicolete to lure young Parrot late at night to steal (she'd say) with her away. But all a ruse it was, of course, just a plot, a plan: a conspiracy to separate Jack from his naïve, unsuspecting silver.

Green like chameleons — that was Jackie Parrot. As green as green could be. In his mind, is was mixed with ought; wouldn't meant won't. Jackie thought want equaled for sure. His mottos were: Innocence is goodness' poof. And: Nothing unpleasant survives inattention.

    Jackie had a lot to learn.

[III]
"Pick from my palette color yellow. Pick from my palette color yellow. Just slide my stiff bow 'long that tight cello."

Yellow was Jackie's gold. And silver and orange, his change. The treasure Nicolete sought to steal for her and blue Beaucaire. The rendezvous was set, Jackie to meet Nicolete in the woods that night, despite the thunderstorm. Gary to jump from the trees and knock Jackie out (or down, at least) and take from Jackie the works of his pocket and the riches of his heart.

"Pick from my paint box, pick color red. Choose from my paint box, choose color red. Shine like a needle hungry for some thread."

Red did flow that stormy nigh while the thunder rolled and the silver lightning flashed. But 'twas the red blood of young Beaucaire, whose blue eyes were beaten the color of Nicol's hair. Even so, Nicolete Gary's true love was, and all her orange-penny noons and all her silver-dime nights rolled forever through Beaucaire's hands.

So Jackie fought and Jackie kept his cash. And Jackie fought and lost his love. And brown like chameleons, did old Jackie grow. And it's the new, mournful Parrot who sings.

"I'm your paintbox, Baby, let me soft-coat you. I'm your paintbox, Sugar, wanna soft-coat you. Want to touch you up 'til you're so squeaky new."

Green like chameleons — that was Jackie Parrot once. As green as green could be. In his mind, is was mixed once with ought; wouldn't meant won't. Once Jackie thought want equaled for sure. His mottos were: Innocence is goodness' poof. And: Nothing unpleasant survives inattention.

    Jackie learned a lot.

```
G I
F T
```

```
the
p o
i s

o n
e r
i s

g o n e
but
her
w o
r k
i s


i n
our
w e
l.l
  x
```

www.ingramcontent.com/pod-product-compliance
Lightning Source LLC
LaVergne TN
LVHW061332060426
835512LV00013B/2609